ND

THE **BACKYARD**

BARTENDER

55 Cool Summer Cocktails

THE BACKYARD

Nicole Aloni

BARTENDER

Clarkson Potter/Publishers
New York

Library of Congress Cataloging-in-Publication
Data is available upon request

ISBN 978-0-307-38105-7

Printed in Singapore

Design by Danielle Deschenes

10 9 8 7 6 5 4 3 2 1

First Edition

CONTENTS

Splash! Sigh! BUZZZZ!

Summer has finally bloomed and the soft, warm air is begging us to slow down, smell the honeysuckle, and perhaps sip something that connects us with the light-hearted side of life. But what? The cocktails that seemed just right when we were shivering by the fire are less than appealing now. Summer drinks must serve a different purpose entirely—they need to be refreshing, bright, and light as sea foam. After all, this is the season when laziness and indulgence become a virtue. What better way to celebrate that easy life than with a fizzy libation?

I had all of those yearnings in mind as this book took shape. My vision for *The Backyard Bartender* is that of a fresh little collection of concoctions to inspire you to pour summer into your glass. These cocktails have all been vigorously tested and enjoyed (it's a dirty job, but someone had to do it). I think you'll love them, too. But please regard them as inspiration for your inner mixologist—and not gospel.

This is the time when we are most reconnected with our gardens and nature. So it's fitting that many of these refreshers have ingredients from the garden and the orchard. Start with spirits you enjoy (infusing some of your own can be lots of fun, see page 102)

Summer is the time when one sheds one's tensions with one's clothes, and the right kind of day is jeweled balm for the battered spirit. A few of those days and you can become drunk with the belief that all's right with the world. —ADA LOUISE HUXTABLE

and experiment with the fresh flavors summer brings—from lavender blossoms to peaches and raspberries—they can all find a place in your shaker. My favorite drinks feature cooling cucumber, tropical fruits, everything from the herb garden, and sugars and spirits with an array of subtle infused flavors. Even if we can't get to the tropics right now (perhaps, especially), we'd definitely like to have a little in our glass.

And if you're one of those people who claim to categorically dislike gin, you may want to sample some of the delicate, soft new products available (see page 105). Gin has definitely become a favorite in my summer bar because of the beautiful way it binds itself to fresh herbs and fruits.

A number of cocktails in this book are delicious and satisfying without alcohol, too. Those recipes are indicated with a ☂. We've also included some original nonalcoholic recipes in Chapter 6.

There are a couple of things to know about summer cocktails (any cocktails, really):

◆ They should be crisply cold. Whenever possible, chill the glass, chill the alcohol, and shake or stir the liquids vigorously on ice before serving. Cold is critical to making alcohol its best!

◆ The very best mixologists know you must carefully measure each component to create great cocktails. To enjoy that 3½ or 4 ounces of nirvana, small quantities of each ingredient must be perfectly balanced. Exceptions might be simple combos like rum and Coke or gin and tonic, but even here it's best to measure so as not to dump in too much alcohol under the mask of those strong mixers. Having watched Tom Cruise in *Cocktail*, you may think that measuring the ingredients for a cocktail is for wimps. Not so!

◆ Cocktails should be easy on the eyes. Drinks have often become popular or famous as much for their appearance as their flavor. So, serve your cocktail in a dewy, pristine glass with a garnish that tells the story of what's in the recipe. Express your creativity by adding a flavored rim to the glass or a garnish that adds another dimension to the flavors in the drink. And, for the giddy time that is summer, I don't know that a tiny plastic elephant or turquoise wiggly worms are out of line as playful adornments.

◆ A cocktail should be compact. They were originally designed to be sipped not gulped. Bah! to supersized cocktails that get you blotto before dinner. *The Classic Measure:* A cocktail should contain no more than 3 ounces of alcohol and no more than five (maybe six) ingredients. The drink shouldn't have more than about 9 ounces of liquid altogether.

So, tip the umbrella to keep the sun out of your eyes, put up your feet, and browse through these pages for scores of ideas about what to stir up this season.

I'd like to send you off with my favorite toast. It's from Mexico, a land of eternal summer.

Salud, amor y pesetas—y tiempo para gustarlos!

(Health, love, and money—and the time to enjoy them.)

Venturing far beyond your grandfather's martini, edgy creative cocktails—including everything from fresh herbs to Asian teas and hand-infused spirits—are definitely hot. Mixologists across the country are expanding the parameters of what might be included in a cocktail glass and people are loving the opportunity to experiment. If you'd like to jump into the cocktail craze, use the following lists to ensure that you've got what it takes.

"The Basic Mixology Bar," page 10, represents the essential purchases for a simple but complete bar. "The Mixologist's Dream Bar," page 11, lists additions to create a bar capable of producing nearly every drink on the scene (and includes some of my favorite brands of spirit).

Since most spirits have a multiyear shelf life, you can conveniently build the collection outlined below over time. As alcohol is a preservative, all spirits will last nearly indefinitely unopened. Opened spirits (like vodka, gin, etc.) will be good for years if stored properly. Some sweet liqueurs (like Midori) really should be consumed within six months of opening. Sherry, port, and other fortified wines may taste stale four to six months after uncorking.

Cocktail party: A gathering held to enable forty people to talk about themselves at the same time. The man who remains after the liquor is gone is the host. —FRED ALLEN

Liquor

Once you determine which spirit(s) appeal to your palate, experiment with different brands. There are distinct levels of quality and complexity within each spirit type. Typically, the premium brands (which naturally always cost more) will have been aged longer and/or have a smoother or more complex taste. All vodkas (and gins, bourbons, etc.) are definitely *not created equal*! Once you've identified your favorites, they will be especially important in straight-up drinks, like a martini or a Manhattan, where the cocktail is simply chilled spirits.

Liquor preferences also have a distinct regional character. New York and the western states consume twice as much vodka as the rest of the country and have a real enthusiasm for tequila. Southern states pour more bourbon, scotch, and gin. So, build your bar with your hometown in mind. And take your personal preferences into account. If you love a Kir, then crème de cassis should be on your Basic Mixology Bar list.

QUANTITIES FOR ENTERTAINING

- **One 750-milliliter bottle of red or white wine equals 4 to 6 glasses.**
- **One-fifth of liquor (25.4 ounces) equals approximately 12 two-ounce measures.**
- **One case of wine equals 60 to 72 five-ounce glasses.**
- **Buy 1 bottle of soda water and mix (i.e., sour mix, Tom Collins, etc.) for every eight guests.**
- **Buy 2 bottles of mineral water for every eight guests.**
- **Buy 1 pound of ice per person.**
- **For a cocktail party, calculate that guests will have two or three cocktails or glasses of wine. For wine served with a formal meal, figure three-quarters of a bottle per person.**

Do not allow children to mix drinks. It is unseemly and they use too much vermouth. —STEVE ALLEN

The Basic Mixology Bar

SPIRITS You should have one 750-milliliter bottle of each of the major types below. Buy the larger size of your favorites; alcohol will keep indefinitely and it is more cost effective in bigger bottles.

Blended scotch	Rum *(light and dark)*
Bourbon	Tequila
Brandy	Vodka
Gin	Whiskey

WINE It's smart to have red and white wine behind the bar for when friends drop by. Select from the popular varietals below. You may want to do a wine-tasting party with your friends to determine your favorites. Then you'll know what to keep on hand in larger quantities.

White Wines	Red Wines
Chardonnay	Cabernet sauvignon
Pinot grigio	Shiraz
Semidry Riesling or Viognier	Pinot noir or merlot

BEER Light
Domestic regular

LIQUEURS Cointreau or triple sec *(orange)*
Amaretto *(almond)*
Kahlúa *(coffee)*
Crème de cacao *(chocolate)*
Crème de menthe *(mint)*
Bailey's Irish Cream *(cream, chocolate, and Irish whiskey)*

APÉRITIFS Campari
Dry vermouth
Sweet vermouth

SPARKLERS Sparkling wine

MIXERS Mineral water
Coco Lopez *(coconut cream)*
Club soda
Cola or diet cola
Ginger ale
7-Up
Grenadine
Tonic
Juices: orange, grapefruit, pineapple, cranberry, and tomato
Frozen lemonade and limeade

GARNISHES & FLAVORINGS Oranges, lemons, and limes (buy these as needed)
Simple syrup *(see page 14)*
Large green olives
Maraschino cherries
Angostura bitters
Tabasco sauce
Worcestershire sauce

The Mixologist's Dream Bar
(À LA NICOLE)

Additions to the Basic Mixologist's Bar

I have included some of my favorite brands where I felt it would be useful.

SPIRITS

Premium vodkas *(like Grey Goose, Ketel One, Wyborowa, and Stolichnaya)*

Orange, vanilla, lemon, and pepper flavored vodkas *(like those from Grey Goose, Absolut, and Stolichnaya)*

Premium rum *(like Myers's, Bacardi, gold and dark)*

Flavored rum *(orange, lemon, and coconut)*

Premium gin *(like Hendrick's, Boodles, Ten, and Bombay Sapphire)*

Single-malt scotch *(like Glenlivet, Laphroaig, Oban, or Lagavulin)*

Premium bourbon *(like Maker's Mark, Woodford Reserve, or Knob Creek)*

Premium whiskey *(like Jack Daniels Single Barrel)*

Gold or añejo tequila *(like Commerativo, Herradura, or Patrón)*

Cachaça *(rum from Brazil)*

Agricole-style rum *(from the West Indies)*

LIQUEURS

Framboise or Chambord *(raspberry)*

Frangelico *(hazelnut)*

Grand Marnier *(orange)*

Pama Liqueur *(pomegranate)*

Godiva Liqueur, White and Dark *(chocolate)*

Limoncello *(lemon)*

Drambuie *(honey-and-herb-flavored whiskey)*

Blue Curaçao *(though blue, its flavor is orange)*

Hpnotiq *(premium vodka, fine cognac, and natural tropical fruit juices with hints of orange and passion fruit)*

FORTIFIED WINES & APERITIFS

Lillet

Dubonnet

(VSOP) Cognac *(like Remy Martin, Bisquit, or Hennessy)*

Fruit brandy *(eau de vie)*—pear, peach, plum, and cherry

Vintage port *(such as Graham's, Warre's, Dow's, and Fonseca)*

Cream sherry

BEERS

Imported *(from Mexico, China, Thailand—the list is endless)*

Microbrews

MIXERS

White cranberry juice

Peach, pear, and other nectars *(preferably Looza brand)*

SPARKLERS

French Champagne

Prosecco *(Italy)*

GARNISHES & FLAVORS

Tamarind paste

Flavored simple syrups

Orange flower water

Peach bitters

Olives stuffed with blue cheese, jalapeño chiles, anchovies, etc.

Lychee fruit

Techniques of the Mixologist

How to Chill a Glass

When making a cocktail, chill the glass *before* adding any liquids. Cool the glass in either the refrigerator or freezer for thirty minutes—or fill it with crushed ice and let it sit for a minute. Always discard the ice and any water from the melted ice before making the cocktail.

How to Frost a Glass

Put the glass in the freezer for at least thirty minutes to frost.

How to Create a Special "Rim"

Wipe the lip of the glass with a lemon or lime wedge to moisten. Press the glass into a saucer filled with a flavoring such as sugar, salt, crushed lemon drops, candied ginger, etc.

How to Use a Cocktail Shaker

Add liquid ingredients to the shaker and fill it three-quarters full with ice cubes. Don't use crushed or cracked ice. After securely attaching the top, hold it in place with one hand while holding the bottom with the other hand. Shake vigorously for ten to fifteen seconds. The shaking motion should be fairly assertive to get the proper effect.

How to Make Lemon or Lime Peel Twists for Garnishes

Use a channel knife (often found as part of a zester) to remove the longest possible strip of peel. Start by pressing the channel into the skin at the top of the lemon and slowly cut around, making a long spiral. Twist into a pig's-tail shape, cut into short sections, or tie the peel into a knot.

How to Blend a Drink

Combine all the liquids in a blender and blend to a puree (if necessary). Add ice (preferably crushed) and blend to the desired consistency. Don't overload the blender with too many cocktails. Typically, only two or three are made in one batch.

How to Make Cracked Ice

Cracked or crushed ice is very useful when making blended drinks. Put ice cubes in a large freezer-weight plastic bag and wrap the bag in a tea towel. Bash the bag evenly with a mallet. If preferred, buy an ice crusher or "macho" blender to do this job.

How to Muddle

Put all ingredients to be muddled (often citrus, herbs, sugar, or lime juice) into the bottom of a shaker or sturdy mixing glass. Use the large or rounded end of a muddler (a wooden mixing spoon works well, too) to crush the ingredients together until fragrant. This simple step will make all the difference in some classic favorites like Mojitos or Caipirinhas because the flavors and aromas that are released in this way are essential. If you are preparing a large batch of a particular drink that requires muddling, a mortar and pestle makes this step easier.

How to Rinse

Many recipes call for a glass to be "rinsed" with a particular liquid. To do this, place a small amount of the liquid in a glass, then swirl it around so that the inside of the glass is evenly coated. Pour any extra liquid out of the glass when done. Dry vermouth is often used to rinse a glass for a "dry" martini.

How to Make a Simple Syrup

Simple syrup is basically liquid sugar created by heating sugar in water until it dissolves. This syrup is essential for wonderful mixology because it eliminates the challenge of dissolving crystal sugar into a cold liquid. Once you learn how to make the syrup, you can easily add a host of herbal and citrus ingredients to create flavored syrups that contribute subtle notes to your cocktails.

For cocktails, I use a ratio of 1 part water to 1 part sugar. Once prepared, the syrup will last for a month or so if well sealed and in the refrigerator.

INSTRUCTIONS

Simple Syrup for Beverages

1 Combine 2 cups of water and 2 cups of granulated sugar in a saucepan. Stir to mix. Place over medium-high heat to dissolve.

2 As soon as the syrup comes to a rolling boil and is completely clear (all of the sugar is dissolved), remove it from the heat. Let it cool and then refrigerate the syrup in a sealed container.

Infused Syrup

1 Add the flavor components as soon as the syrup is removed from the heat by pushing them all the way to the bottom of the pan. Cover the mixture and let it steep for 30 to 40 minutes.

2 Pour the syrup through a fine sieve, pressing down firmly on the flavoring to extract all the juice into the syrup.

3 Store the syrup in a covered container in the refrigerator for up to a month.

Great Flavoring Additions for Simple Syrup

◆ 4 lemons, washed and finely sliced (keep them submerged by placing a plate on top of them during the infusing process)
◆ ¾ cup peeled, minced gingerroot
◆ 1 cup chopped fresh mint leaves
◆ 1 cup chopped fresh basil leaves
◆ ¼ cup minced fresh rosemary
◆ ½ cup dried lavender

Tools of the Mixologist

Basic Glassware

Over the decades some very lovely glasses have been created for specific drinks that can add a lot to the appearance and enjoyment of the cocktail—think cactus-stemmed margarita glass. However, only a few basic styles are necessary while easing into full mixology madness.

Martini Glasses

It is essential to have this glass for any drink styling itself as a martini. The wide-open face and graceful stem show off the pretty drink and keep hot hands away from the cold liquid. I suggest having these glasses in both a 4- to 5-ounce size for martinis and other cocktails served "up" and an 8- to 9-ounce size for blended drinks and "Dessert in a Glass" drinks (see page 95). These should be clear—not colored—with perhaps a small design and nothing more. Note: In a new trend reflecting mixologists' continual striving for innovation, some stylish martinis are being served in glasses without stems.

Rocks or Old-fashioned Glasses

The short, stubby all-purpose bar glass with straight sides and a heavy bottom is used for anything "on the rocks" and works well for muddled drinks such as Caipirinhas or for medium-sized drinks like the Negroni or Fuzzy Italian.

(continued)

Cocktail ABCs

◆ **All drinks are meant to be *served immediately* after preparing, with the exception of the beverages in the "Cocktails for a Crowd" chapter. (These are especially designed to be all, or mostly all, prepared and chilled ahead of time to eliminate last-minute party hassles.)**

◆ **All drinks that are chilled in a cocktail shaker with ice should be shaken for 10 to 15 seconds. A few cocktails require vigorous agitation to create a foamy texture or to break down fresh ingredients. For those recipes, the word *vigorously* appears in the instructions.**

◆ **When a shaker is used, it should always be filled three-quarters full with ice cubes (not chipped or crushed ice).**

◆ **All cocktails served "up" (without ice) should be served in a chilled glass (see page 12).**

◆ **If a special rim is to be added to the lip of the glass, always do this after the glass has been chilled.**

Highball or Collins Glasses

These glasses have tall, straight sides and are perfectly designed to hold lots of ice and plenty of refreshing liquids like tonic, soda, or ginger ale. Everything in this book's "Coolers" chapter can be served in one of these glasses. They come in many sizes; but I like ones with very clean lines that are about 6 to 7 inches tall and hold about 8 to 10 ounces of liquid.

Champagne Flutes

This glass is perfectly crafted to bring out the best in your bubbly. The long, narrow bowl keeps the bubbles from escaping and the long stem keeps warm hands away from the Champagne. In fine crystal versions, there may even be a tiny bubble blown into the bottom of the bowl to stimulate the continuous, enticing release of bubbles up the glass. Do not think of serving Champagne in any other glass (unless you're drinking it out of a slipper).

Special Glasses

As you become more adept at and devoted to your bar, you may wish to acquire some of the following additional glassware styles:

Brandy snifters	Pilsners
Goblets	Sherry or aperitif glasses
Margarita glasses	Sour glasses
Milkshake glasses	

SOME USEFUL LIQUID MEASUREMENTS

¼ ounce= ½ tablespoon	2 ounces= ¼ cup
½ ounce= 1 tablespoon	4 ounces= ½ cup
1 ounce= 2 tablespoons	8 ounces= 1 cup
1 jigger= 1½ ounces	

Bar Spoon

A long-handled spoon for mixing and measuring; the flat side can be used for muddling. You will use this spoon for many drinks and it's definitely one of those tools that makes you feel like a pro.

Bar Strainer

This metal, paddle-shaped device fits onto the top of a tumbler or shaker to strain the liquid into the glass while keeping out the bits of ice, herbs, or citrus. I think it is much more effective than the little strainer built into the top of the can-style shakers. Plus, you will use this strainer for stirred and sometimes even blended drinks to keep chunks of ice out of the cocktail glass.

Blender

A sturdy, powerful blender is a "must" for any bar. What's important here is horsepower. The number of speed adjustments isn't significant.

Champagne Stopper

The metal stopper with two locking wings is used to reseal a bottle of Champagne. This is fairly effective at keeping the bubbles in the bottle for a day or so. But, honestly, when opening a bottle of Champagne, it's best to count on serving the whole thing that day.

Channel Knife

Cuts a long, fairly thick strip of citrus peel with some pith to make into twists and other garnishes. This is by far the simplest way to create the ubiquitous cocktail twists.

Cocktail Shaker

A stainless-steel or glass container used to mix and chill drinks. A number of different effects can be achieved with the vigorous use of a shaker. Flavors can simply be blended and chilled, herbs can be infused into the liquids, or tiny shards of ice can be introduced into a martini for desired bruising. Most pros prefer a Boston shaker, which has a large mixing glass on top of the mixing can. But the all-metal type with a built-in strainer and cap works well, too.

Corkscrew

There's not too much call for these when making cocktails. But it's best to have one on hand for sangrias or for wine-loving friends. Many quality styles are available.

Ice Mallet

Used to make crushed ice from ice cubes for drinks such as the Mojito.

Muddler

A wandlike tool (similar to a mortar in chemistry), rounded at one end, about 6 to 8 inches long, and usually made of wood or porcelain, a muddler is used to crush and mix ingredients such as herbs or citrus wedges in a shaker or glass. Since the massive popularity of Mojitos began, Rösle has come out with a new stainless-steel/plastic muddler that is both handsome and easy to use.

Jigger Measure

A jigger (also called a shot glass) is a petite measuring cup designed just for cocktails. To create excellent cocktails, all ingredients must be measured, and this little guy will be essential. Jiggers come in a variety of styles: There are silver hourglass-shaped ones with a 1-ounce measure on one end and a 2-ounce measure on the other end as well as the glass measuring cups that indicate quantities from $\frac{1}{2}$ ounce to 4 ounces on the side, which I particularly like. Make sure to have several.

Mixing (or Pint) Glasses

These glasses are useful for assembling drinks like Manhattans that are stirred, not shaken. They can also be used to muddle a double or triple batch of Caipirinhas or Mojitos.

Zester

A Microplane zester is a wonderful tool and will easily yield lovely, filmy strands of citrus zest to add a gentle layer of flavor to any cocktail.

The Lemon Drop, page 21

3 | **MARTINI** MADNESS

H.L. Mencken once called the martini "the only American invention as perfect as the sonnet."

Martinis were invented in the late 1800s and have gone wildly in and out of fashion ever since. For the last fifteen years or so, they have been enjoying a vogue in flavored, colored, and bejeweled variations that would have astonished exacting martini connoisseurs—all pretty much inflamed by the *Sex and the City* passion for Cosmos. This new range of more complex, sometimes sweeter flavors has given the cocktail a far broader appeal.

Martinis could become a very cool theme for a casual summer bash. To throw a successful martini party, set up a self-serve Martini Buffet with recipes and ingredients for three or four contrasting martinis. Guests will try their hand at preparing their own cocktails while you serve well-matched hors d'oeuvres. Garnishes, such as lemon twists, and any special ingredients (see Simple Syrup, page 14) should be prepared beforehand.

The Self-Serve Martini Buffet

1 Rent or borrow enough martini glasses so it won't be necessary to wash glasses between tastings. Use small glasses since guests will be sampling, not gulping.

2 Decorate one large (or two small) buffet tables for the martini setup.

3 For each martini, provide a shaker, a printed recipe, ingredients, garnishes, and glasses.

4 Put the liquor for each martini on ice. Have a separate bowl of ice for use in the shaker.

5 Scatter bowls of spicy nuts or cheese straws around the room. Offer three or four warm hors d'oeuvres that complement the flavors of the selected martinis, bringing out the hors d'oeuvres one tray at a time.

Why don't you get out of that wet coat and into a dry martini? —ROBERT BENCHLEY

How to Make a Great Martini

Technique

All steps are meant to create the two essential conditions of a perfect martini: The drink must be as *cold* as possible and there should be as *little melted ice* (water) as possible in the drink.

◆ Chill glasses.
◆ Fill the shaker three-quarters full with ice cubes and add the liquid ingredients. Replace the top, gripping it with one hand; hold the can with your other hand. Shake up and down vigorously to mix and chill for 10 to 15 seconds.
◆ Immediately strain into chilled glasses.

Essential Equipment

18-ounce shaker (This essential tool comes in two basic styles. The Boston shaker, preferred by most professional bartenders, is a metal cup topped with a pint mixing glass. All-metal shakers typically have a strainer built into the lid. Both work well.)

4- to 5-ounce martini glasses (see page 14)
Ice bucket
Plenty of ice (1 pound for four cocktails or per guest)
Premium liquor

Fun Extras

◆ Small vermouth atomizer—a tiny mister for applying the merest whisper of vermouth to a martini glass (for a really "dry" martini)
◆ Stuffed olives (such as blue cheese, anchovy, jalapeño)
◆ Unusual olive-garnish picks

A single cocktail should consist of no more than 2½ to 3 ounces of alcohol. So, 4- or 5-ounce martini glasses allow you to serve cocktails in the moderate portions originally intended. The whole supersized trend of the American food scene is really out of place at the cocktail bar.

Because a martini is essentially "liquor drunk neat," the quality of the spirit is of utmost importance. A lesser brand might be wonderful in a "cooler" with lots of juice and soda, but not in the pristine martini or Manhattan.

I hate to advocate drugs, alcohol, violence or insanity to anyone, but they've always worked for me. —HUNTER S. THOMPSON

LEMON DROP MARTINI
MAKES 1 • *Photograph on page 18*

GLASS:	Chilled martini
RIM:	Superfine sugar or crushed lemon drop candies. (Superfine sugar may be purchased or made by grinding regular sugar in a spice grinder.)
GARNISH:	Lemon peel twists

The lemon drop became a fad in California in the 1970s as one of the first "girlie" martinis; it has remained one of the most popular. For those of us who like sour candy and lemon tarts, this is the best.

2 lemon wedges

¾ teaspoon simple syrup (see page 14)

1½ ounces Absolut Citron vodka

½ ounce Cointreau

1 Rub the rim of the glass with a lemon wedge. Press the glass into a saucer of superfine sugar.

2 Put the lemon wedges and simple syrup in a cocktail shaker and muddle well. Add the vodka and Cointreau. Fill with ice.

3 Shake *vigorously* to chill.

4 Strain the mixture into the chilled glass. Garnish.

THE DEEP END
MAKES 1

This refreshing citrus cocktail will remind you of the shimmering, endless, icy blue of an Infinity Pool. Blue Curaçao adds a kiss of orange flavor and the elusive blue that makes this cocktail so appealing. This gorgeous color can be reproduced by substituting 3 ounces of Hpnotiq (essentially a cocktail in a bottle) for all of the liquids except the bitters. This is one of those recipes that just isn't the same without a little dash of bitters.

2 ounces premium gin (like Plymouth or Hendrick's)

½ ounce Cointreau

1 ounce Rose's lime juice

Splash (¼ teaspoon) Blue Curaçao

Dash of Angostura bitters

1 **Fill a cocktail shaker three-quarters full with ice.**

2 **Add the gin, Cointreau, lime juice, and Blue Curaçao.**

3 **Shake and strain into the chilled glass.**

4 **Add a dash of bitters. Garnish.**

 The Backyard Bartender

One martini is alright, two is too many, and three is not enough. —JAMES THURBER

CAJUN HEAT MARTINI
MAKES 2

GLASS: Chilled martini
GARNISH: 2 pickled jalapeño peppers

The idea of a fiery martini seems to have emerged from the Cajun-influenced kitchens of New Orleans. Prepare this spicy drink with commercial pepper vodka or create your own pepper-infused vodka or gin (see "Infusing Spirits," page 102).

6 ounces pepper vodka (Absolut Peppar or homemade)

1 ounce dry vermouth

Dash of Peychaud bitters, optional

1 Fill a cocktail shaker three-quarters full with ice. Add the pepper vodka and the dry vermouth.

2 Shake well. Strain into each chilled glass.

3 Add bitters, if desired, on top of each drink. Garnish.

 The Backyard Bartender

TAMARINDO

MAKES 1

GLASS: Chilled martini
RIM: Orange wedge and ginger sugar
(1 tablespoon of sugar mixed with
¼ teaspoon ground ginger)
GARNISH: Kumquat half or lychee fruit

Tamarind contributes the tangy fruit flavor popular in many Asian and Middle Eastern dishes. Combined here with orange, ginger, and mango, it creates a memorable, vividly tropical summer martini, and the caramel color is intriguing.

2 ounces orange vodka (like Grey Goose L'Orange)

1½ ounces tamarind puree (available at Asian markets)

1 ounce mango nectar (preferably Looza brand)

½ ounce ginger simple syrup (see page 14)

1 Wipe the rim of a chilled glass with an orange wedge. Press the glass into a saucer of ginger sugar.

2 Fill a cocktail shaker three-quarters full with ice.

3 Add the vodka, tamarind puree, mango nectar, and ginger simple syrup to the shaker. Shake *vigorously* to chill.

4 Strain into the prepared glass. Garnish.

THE **KISS**
MAKES 2

GLASS: Chilled martini
GARNISH: 2 orange peel strips or Hershey's kisses

Clear as a Steuben vase and as chocolate-y as a French truffle, this is a decadent treat for those who find a traditional martini overpowering. And it's great as an after-dinner treat.

2 ounces bittersweet chocolate

4 ounces Stoli Vanil vodka or vanilla-infused vodka (see page 102)

4 ounces white crème de cacao

1 On a microwave-safe saucer, melt the chocolate gently in a microwave in 30-second increments.

2 Dip each glass rim into the saucer of melted chocolate and swirl to coat the lip. (For a party, this can be done up to several hours ahead, setting aside the glasses on the counter—in which case they will not be chilled.)

3 Fill a cocktail shaker three-quarters full with ice. Add the vodka and crème de cacao. Shake for 15 seconds to chill.

4 Strain the very cold liquid into the chilled glass —it will magically become crystal clear as it settles. Garnish; if using kisses, drop them into the glasses.

Forget love...I'd rather fall in chocolate.
—ANONYMOUS

The Kiss

Espresso Martini with a Twist,
page 28

ESPRESSO MARTINI
WITH A TWIST
MAKES 4

GLASS: Chilled martini
GARNISH: 12 chocolate-covered coffee beans and 4 long lemon peel twists

A student suggested this elegant cocktail to me when she said, "I love espresso and martinis; couldn't they be in the same glass?" As it turns out, this energizing union is absolutely addictive and has become a favorite everywhere I teach.

This recipe is for four drinks since you need to prepare a batch of coffee.

6 ounces vodka

6 ounces Kahlúa

4 ounces white crème de cacao

4 ounces chilled, double-strength espresso

1 Fill a cocktail shaker with ice.

2 Add half of the vodka, Kahlúa, crème de cacao, and espresso.

3 Shake well. The mixture will become foamy.

4 Pour the mixture into 2 chilled martini glasses and drop in 3 coffee beans per glass. Garnish with lemon peel.

5 Repeat for 2 more cocktails.

The Backyard Bartender

THE **GARDENER**
MAKES 1

GLASS: Chilled martini
GARNISH: Lemon peel or one sprig of rosemary

Include lemon and fresh herbs in a shaker to create a simple martini with all of the pale green promise of an early summer garden.

Dash of dry vermouth

2 ounces vodka (like Grey Goose)

Sprig of rosemary or thyme leaves

1 large piece lemon peel

2 ounces fresh lemonade (preferably homemade), optional

1 **Rinse the glass with dry vermouth, discarding the leftover vermouth (see page 13).**

2 **Fill a cocktail shaker three-quarters full with ice.**

3 **Add the vodka, rosemary, lemon peel, and lemonade, if desired. Shake *vigorously* to infuse and chill.**

4 **Strain into the chilled glass. Garnish.**

U-PICK RASPBERRY
MARTINI
MAKES 1

GLASS: Chilled martini
GARNISH: Fresh raspberry

Lisa Dupar owns a popular restaurant in Red-
mond, Washington (just outside Seattle),
called Pomegranate Bistro. However, she is
probably best known as Seattle's premier
caterer. This vividly hued martini is both a
signature for Lisa's company and a lovely
way to enjoy some of Washington's great
berry crop.

1 ½ ounces premium vodka
8 or 9 freshly picked summer raspberries
½ ounce cranberry juice
½ ounce simple syrup (see page 14)
½ ounce sweet red vermouth
Squeeze of lime

1 Fill a cocktail shaker with ice.

2 Add the vodka, raspberries, cranberry juice,
simple syrup, vermouth, and lime to the shaker.

3 Shake *vigorously* and strain into the chilled
glass. Garnish.

KEY LIME PIE

MAKES 2

GLASS: Chilled martini or parfait

RIM: Caramel sauce and 2 tablespoons crushed graham cracker crumbs

GARNISH: Lime wheel or twist

This simple concoction magically re-creates the flavor of Key lime pie in a martini glass. Make a pitcher of these for your next backyard cookout. You might even add a dollop of whipped cream and offer a second one of these for dessert.

3 ounces Stoli Vanil vodka or vanilla-infused vodka (see page 102)

3 ounces light rum

2 tablespoons fresh lime juice

3 tablespoons cream of coconut (like Coco Lopez)

1 Dip the rim of a martini or parfait glass into the caramel sauce. Then press the glass into a saucer of graham cracker crumbs to coat.

2 In a shaker with lots of ice, combine the vodka, rum, lime juice, and cream of coconut. Shake to blend and chill. Strain into the rimmed glasses. Garnish.

THE **WILLAMETTE**

MAKES 1 • *Photograph on page 112*

Named for the gorgeous Willamette Valley in Oregon, which produces beautiful berries and some of the world's great pinot noirs, this deeply hued drink will elicit *oohs* from your guests even before they taste it! Berry purees are available at specialty stores or can be made by pureeing the fruit and then straining out the tiny seeds.

2½ ounces vodka

2 tablespoons blackberry or marionberry puree

½ ounce lavender simple syrup (see page 14)

½ ounce fresh lime juice

1 **In a shaker with ice, combine the vodka, puree, simple syrup, and lime juice.**

2 **Shake to chill and strain into the chilled martini glass. Garnish.**

THE PERFECT **COSMO**
MAKES 1

GLASS: Chilled martini
GARNISH: Lime wheel

This is the classic recipe created in New York in the late '80s that went on to bodacious acclaim as the drink of choice for the stars of *Sex and the City*. The Cosmopolitan is slightly less alcoholic than many other martini variations. That and its tart, citrusy flavor have also contributed to its widespread popularity.

1½ ounces Absolut Citron vodka or lemon-infused vodka (see page 102)

½ ounce Cointreau

1 ounce cranberry juice

½ ounce fresh lime juice

1 Fill a cocktail shaker three-quarters full with ice. Add the vodka, Cointreau, cranberry juice, and lime juice.

2 Shake to chill.

3 Strain into the chilled glass. Garnish.

Classic Margarita,
page 37

Even though a number of people
have tried, no one has ever found
a way to drink for a living.
—JEAN KERR

4 | **CLASSIC** COCKTAILS

For the purposes of this book, we have defined *classics* as any drink that was popular before 1960 and that is still popular today. Some cocktails have achieved an *evergreen* status: They just keep on being ordered year after year. These drinks may not reflect the latest trends, but their flavor profile has proven to be appealing to so many for so long that you really should know how to make them.

These recipes are also important because they are the foundation for 99.9 percent of the trendy beverages around today. Once you understand the proportions and balance of sweet/sour/spirit in these, you have the structure for an unlimited variety of inventions.

PIÑA COLADA
MAKES 1

GLASS: Chilled goblet or tall
GARNISH: Orange wheel or pineapple wedge and a straw

The piña colada, which was created in Puerto Rico, means "strained pineapple." When blended correctly, it is a consistent, creamy white. With its delicate pineapple-coconut flavor, the piña colada is one of the most popular tropical drinks ever.

Popular variations of this "classic" include mango, papaya, banana, and strawberry.

1½ ounces light rum

1½ ounces cream of coconut (like Coco Lopez)

3 ounces pineapple juice or crushed pineapple

1 ounce fresh lime juice

½ ounce simple syrup (see page 14)

1 cup ice

1 good grate of fresh nutmeg

1 **In a blender combine the rum, cream of coconut, pineapple juice, lime juice, and simple syrup.**

2 **Blend until smooth.**

3 **Add ice and process until smooth again.**

4 **Pour into a large glass. Dust with nutmeg, garnish, and add a straw.**

 The Backyard Bartender

CLASSIC MARGARITA
MAKES 4 ● *Photograph on page 34*

GLASS: Chilled margarita or martini
RIM: Lime wedge and coarse or margarita salt
GARNISH: Lime wheels or wedges

I grew up in Southern California, where margaritas (and tequila) were ubiquitous. Hence, I feel very strongly about the correct way to enjoy one of these tart refreshers. It is essential to serve this great cocktail "on the rocks," as it was created—not blended into a slushy concoction. The additional choices about whether to use Cointreau or Grand Marnier for the orange component and/or white or gold tequila are very much a matter of personal preference. My favorite is gold tequila and Grand Marnier. Freshly squeezed lime juice is essential.

The margarita was most likely created in a Mexican border town (like Tijuana) in the 1930s or '40s, but it's hard to know. A number of folks claim to have invented this lovely drink. All we know for sure is that it transformed tequila from an unknown spirit into a player on the American bar scene.

Popular variations of this "classic" are the Cadillac (made with Grand Marnier), blended, strawberry, pineapple, and ginger.

½ cup fresh lime juice

¾ cup good-quality tequila (gold or white, depending on taste)

¼ cup Grand Marnier or Cointreau

1 **Moisten glass rims with a lime wedge. Press each rim into a saucer of coarse salt to coat. If using fine tequila, it's traditional to salt only half of the rim so that the tequila may be enjoyed without the masking effect of the salt. Slip a lime wedge over the rim.**

2 **In a pitcher filled with ice, combine the lime juice, tequila, and Grand Marnier or Cointreau. Stir to blend and chill. Strain into the prepared glasses. (Add ice to the glass if preferred.)**

AMARETTO SOUR
MAKES 1

GLASS: Chilled sour glass, bistro glass, or champagne flute

GARNISH: Orange wheel and/or a fresh cherry

The nutty flavor of Amaretto is perfectly complemented by the citrus additions in this glass. This is perennially one of the most popular cocktails because it is flat-out yummy. Popular variations of this "classic" are whiskey, peach, and pear sours.

2 ounces Amaretto liqueur

1 ounce fresh lemon juice

1 ounce simple syrup (see page 14)

2 ounces fresh orange juice

1 Fill a cocktail shaker three-quarters full with ice.

2 Add the Amaretto, lemon juice, simple syrup, and orange juice. Shake well to chill.

3 Strain into the chilled glass. Garnish.

Amaretto Sour (left) and Ramos Fizz

RAMOS FIZZ

MAKES 2

Also known as the New Orleans Fizz, this is one of the oldest cocktails, having appeared on the scene in the late 1800s. It's still one of the loveliest for a special occasion when you want to serve a delicate, refreshing alcoholic beverage early in the day. Many people feel that a wedding shower or summer brunch of any variety is incomplete without a pitcher of Ramos. You need a good blender to get these perfectly frothy. You can feel free to omit the raw egg if you're concerned about the health risks.

3 ounces gin

¼ cup half-and-half

1 ounce fresh lemon juice

1 ounce fresh lime juice

1 egg white

2 tablespoons powdered or superfine sugar (may be purchased or made by grinding regular sugar in a spice grinder)

½ cup cracked ice

2 large strips of fresh orange peel (or a dash of orange flower water)

1 **Add the gin, half-and-half, lemon juice, lime juice, egg white, sugar, and ice to a blender.**

2 *Vigorously* **twist the orange peel over the ingredients to release the orange oil into the container.**

3 **Use the same piece of peel to rub around the rim of each serving glass.**

4 **Blend the ingredients until creamy and frothy.**

5 **Pour the drink into glasses. Garnish.**

If you were to ask me if I'd ever had the bad luck to miss my daily cocktail, I'd have to say that I doubt it. Where certain things are concerned, I plan ahead. —LUIS BUÑUEL

SIDECAR
MAKES 1

GLASS: Martini, Dubonnet, or rocks
RIM: lemon juice and sugar
GARNISH: Orange peel or lemon twist

The sidecar was the first cocktail that ever caught my fancy and it remains a favorite. It is said to have been invented at Harry's Bar in Paris (the source of many great cocktails). For a delicious update, replace the brandy with Poire William (pear brandy) or calvados (apple brandy).

2 ounces premium brandy
½ ounce Cointreau
½ ounce fresh lemon juice

1 Rub the rim of the glass with a little of the lemon juice, then press it into a saucer of sugar.

2 Fill a cocktail shaker three-quarters full with ice.

3 Add the brandy, Cointreau, and lemon juice. Shake to chill.

4 Strain into the prepared glass. Garnish.

MANHATTAN
MAKES 1

GLASS: Chilled martini
GARNISH: Maraschino cherry

There are many tales surrounding the naming of this drink (including one involving an Indian tribe local to Manhattan, early explorers, and firewater). Anything that has been around this long, with this many devotees, is bound to have attracted some urban legends.

People who drink Manhattans (like aficionados of other straight-up drinks, such as martinis and sidecars) are very picky. Measurements must be precise and the bourbon their favorite, or something that was a delight is *awful*. To make it even more challenging, there are three common variations on the Manhattan: Perfect (a little of everything), Dry, or Sweet. Included here is the one that is most popular on the bar scene today (Sweet) along with the bourbon that is most often called for.

2 ounces Maker's Mark Bourbon

1 ounce sweet vermouth (for a cool update, replace the vermouth with red Dubonnet)

1 to 3 dashes of Angostura bitters

1 Fill a pint mixing glass with ice.

2 Add the bourbon, vermouth, and bitters to the glass and stir quickly to chill.

3 Strain into the chilled martini glass and garnish.

DAIQUIRI
MAKES 1

GLASS: Chilled martini or sour
GARNISH: Lime wheel

The warm climate and the availability of good local rum and great fruit seem to have provided Cuba with a flood of inspiration for summer quaffs that have become classics. Drinks that were invented in Cuba include the Mojito, the Cuba Libre, and the daiquiri.

After the Spanish-American War, a team of American engineers spent some summer months in the little mining town of Daiquiri, Cuba. According to tradition, it was this group who first shook up rum, lime, and sugar into a boldly refreshing cocktail. As with the margarita, many variations have been created since the original became popular. Sometimes daiquiris are blended with ice, and a wide range of fruits have also been added to the formula, but this is the original.

2½ ounces light rum

1 ounce fresh grapefruit juice

½ ounce simple syrup (see page 14)

½ ounce fresh lime juice

1 Fill a cocktail shaker three-quarters full with ice.

2 Add the rum, grapefruit juice, simple syrup, and lime juice to the shaker.

3 Shake well to chill.

4 Strain into the chilled glass. Garnish.

EL FLORIDITA #3
MAKES 1

GLASS: Chilled sour or martini
GARNISH: Wide grapefruit peel and a maraschino cherry

This daiquiri variation is from noted Portland, Oregon, mixologist Ryan Magarian. He feels that any of the Agricole rums bring a subtler, more complex note to the daiquiri (unlike most rums, Agricole is made from sugarcane and not molasses). This is said to be the recipe Papa Hemingway enjoyed.

2 ounces 10 Cane Agricole-style rum (available at good liquor stores)

¼ ounce Maraska Maraschino Croatia Original liqueur

¾ ounce fresh lime juice

½ ounce fresh grapefruit juice

½ ounce simple syrup (see page 14)

1 Fill a cocktail shaker three-quarters full with ice.

2 Add all ingredients to the shaker and shake to chill.

3 Strain the drink into the chilled glass. Garnish.

Daiquiri

Ice can be so much more than just that little cube of coldness that makes your tea or Negroni taste more refreshing. Below are some special ice recipes to bring cold, beautiful, and flavorful together in one crunchy little package.

Some of these suggestions pack more flavor punch than others, but they all bring more to a beverage than just a drop in the temperature. Adding flavored cubes to tall, warm-weather beverages like iced tea, Lavender Lushes, or Mojitos will ensure that the drink isn't getting watered down while it's being cooled down. For individual cubes of note, fill ice cube trays with:

1 **Lime juice and a sliver of jalapeño in each cube (for sangrita or spicy margaritas).**
2 **Lemonade and a raspberry in each cube (for lemonade, iced tea, or a Lemon Breeze).**
3 **Pink lemonade and a rose or nasturtium petal (for *Agua Fresca*, Ipanema Punch, or iced tea).**
4 **Sweetened coffee and a sliver of lemon peel (for iced coffee).**
5 **Sweetened water or 7-Up and mint leaves (for iced tea or a Strawberry Shirley).**

Another great solution to chilling without diluting is to create ice from the beverage itself. This is especially effective when serving from a punch bowl. Freeze punch, lemonade, or tea in a dessert mold, Bundt pan, or coffee can. Add lemon-peel slices, cherries, or mint leaves in a pretty pattern and use the resulting ice art to chill and decorate the punch bowl.

Custom Arctic Ice Bucket

Ice can also be employed to make a statement on a more dramatic scale. Construct a *wow* centerpiece for the bar by making a decorated ice bucket from solid ice to chill the champagne, wine, or vodka bottles used to make your crisp, cold cocktails.

**INSTRUCTIONS FOR MAKING
A CUSTOM ARCTIC ICE BUCKET**

Find two large metal cans that fit inside one another with at least a 1-inch gap (like a no. 10 can and a 1-pound coffee can). Make sure the inner can is large enough to hold a wine bottle.

1 **Pour 1 inch of water in the larger can and freeze it solid. (For a crystal-clear cooler, use distilled water.)**

2 **Place the smaller can on the layer of ice in the larger can. Use strips of duct tape across the top of the cans to secure the smaller can directly in the center of the larger can. Put a weight (such as a can of peas) in the smaller can.**

3 **Place this assembly on a small tray to make it easier to move. Fill the space between the two cans with water and fronds of lacy dill, fern leaves, lemon wheels, or long-stemmed roses. Freeze until solid, 4 to 8 hours.**

4 **After removing the weight and duct tape, briefly immerse the larger can in warm water to unmold the ice. Put hot water in the smaller can to remove it from the center.**

5 **Put this pretty "ice bucket" on a shallow tray or platter to catch the drips. Slip in a bottle of your favorite beverage. Place display glasses and garnishes around it.**

Cheers!

Sangrita Rooster Tail,
page 48

5 | **SOON-TO-BE** CLASSICS

In recent years cocktails have become as inventive, seasonal, and reflective of the excitement to be found in blending world cuisines as any part of the food scene. In this chapter you'll find new recipes that I believe have the potential to become the next "Wow" cocktail. They are beautiful to look at, include unusual ingredients in unique combinations, and have elicited consistent "oohs and ahs" from my tasting panel. Any one of these drinks could become your signature cocktail. Mix on!

Chocolate Citron, page 52

SANGRITA ROOSTER TAIL

MAKES 2

GLASS: Highball and shot
GARNISH: Fresh jalapeño or serrano chile and a sprinkle of cumin

This is a traditional Mexican drink that deserves to be more popular. A Rooster Tail is the perfect occasion to bring out that bottle of aged tequila you brought back from your last trip to Mexico—something like Commerativo or Herradura. This is a two-part cocktail, so let guests know that they should first enjoy a sip of the very refreshing sangrita, then follow that with a sip of tequila. Olé!

For the sangrita

⅓ cup tomato juice

    Juice of ½ lime

⅔ cup fresh orange juice

½ teaspoon sugar

1 to 2 dashes Tabasco sauce

    Premium tequila to taste

1 **Mix all of the sangrita ingredients and chill them for at least 2 hours.**

2 **Serve the sangrita in highball glasses garnished with a fresh chile pepper and the cumin.**

3 **Serve the tequila in shot glasses beside the rosy sangrita.**

Served by itself, sangrita is a wonderful nonalcoholic drink.

HOT STUFF
MAKES 1

GLASS: Martini

RIM: Lime wedge and hot sugar (1 tablespoon sugar mixed with ⅛ to ¼ teaspoon cayenne pepper and ¼ teaspoon ground ginger)

GARNISH: Jalapeño and star fruit slices

The tequila *float* mingles with the spicy rim to take your breath away. The cool citrus of the cocktail then soothes as it rushes down your throat. A must for those who love good tequila and a little spice in their life.

2 ounces Absolut Citron or lemon-infused vodka (see page 102)

1 ounce fresh lime juice

¾ ounce lemon simple syrup (see page 14)

½ ounce premium gold tequila

1 Fill a cocktail shaker three-quarters full with ice.

2 Combine the lemon vodka, lime juice, and lemon simple syrup in the shaker. Shake to chill.

3 Strain the beverage into the glass rimmed with the lime wedge and the hot sugar mixture.

4 Pour the tequila over the back of a spoon to slowly drizzle it onto the surface of the drink. Garnish.

TEN THYME SMASH

MAKES 1

GLASS: Chilled martini
GARNISH: Thyme sprig

Ryan Magarian is a friend and one of the country's most renowned mixologists. He takes cocktails to another level, introducing a chef's palate and sensibilities to his cocktail recipes. This lovely drink is typical of Ryan's preference for elegantly blended flavors.

2 thin slices of cucumber
2 sprigs of fresh thyme
2 ounces Aviation or Ten gin
¾ ounce fresh lime juice
½ ounce white cranberry juice
½ ounce simple syrup (see page 14)

1 **In a pint shaker glass, muddle the cucumber and the 2 sprigs of fresh thyme.**
2 **Add the gin, lime juice, cranberry juice, and simple syrup with lots of ice and shake.**
3 **Strain the drink into the glass. Garnish.**

POMEGRANATE SMACK

MAKES 1

GLASS: Chilled martini
RIM: Pomegranate molasses and sugar
GARNISH: Kumquat or star fruit slice

The Smack showcases the exotic and seductive taste of pomegranate molasses—one of the decade's new super ingredients found in everything from salad dressing to cheesecake. This zingy martini was created by Matt Skeel, the gifted bar manager at Serafina restaurant in Seattle.

3 ounces vodka

1 tablespoon pomegranate molasses

½ ounce fresh lemon juice

1 tablespoon simple syrup (see page 14)

Splash of soda water, optional

1 Use your finger to smear a thin coating of the pomegranate molasses on the rim of the glass. Press the rim into a saucer of sugar.

2 Fill a cocktail shaker three-quarters full with ice.

3 Add the vodka, pomegranate molasses, lemon juice, and simple syrup. Shake to chill.

4 Strain the drink into the chilled glass. Garnish.

CHOCOLATE CITRON
MAKES 1

GLASS: Chilled martini
RIM: Dark or white chocolate (SPECIAL OPTION: Press minced, candied ginger into the chocolate on the rim while still soft— whooeee!)
GARNISH: Lemon peel twist

The clear notes of lemon and chocolate in this cocktail are a definite *wow!* It drinks as if you're slurping down a chocolate-covered lemon bar.

1 ounce Limoncello liqueur (from the freezer)

1 ounce Absolut Citron vodka

1 ounce dark chocolate liqueur (like Godiva)

1 Melt the chocolate on a saucer in the microwave in 30-second increments just until it liquefies (usually about 30 seconds).

2 Roll the rim of the glass in the melted chocolate and let it set for 1 to 2 minutes (or up to 2 hours).

3 Fill a cocktail shaker with ice.

4 Add the Limoncello, vodka, and chocolate liqueur to the shaker and shake to chill.

5 Strain the drink into the chilled glass. Garnish.

Il Jardin, page 56

6 | COOLERS AND
TROPICAL COCKTAILS

Likely the original "cooler" was some version of a gin and tonic sucked down for medicinal purposes by a sunburned Englishman in the late 1870s. Today coolers have become one of the most popular types of summer beverages for obvious reasons; they're tall and cooling, with lots of ice and mixer and relatively little alcohol—just what you need to feel refreshed while spending an afternoon by the pool or mingling at a garden party.

The correct glass for the drinks in this chapter will be a tall or Collins glass but any tumbler can work. Many of the following elixirs are also delicious without the alcohol. These are indicated with a 🍹.

IL JARDIN

MAKES 1 • *Photograph on page 54*

Cilantro adds a lovely exotic flavor to this yummy tequila cooler. If you're not a fan of cilantro, mint can be used instead. When shaken *vigorously* this turns frothy/creamy like a Ramos Fizz.

2 ounces tequila

4 or 5 cilantro leaves

½ ounce triple sec

½ ounce simple syrup (preferably lemon, see page 14)

3 ounces pineapple juice

Soda water to top

1 Fill a cocktail shaker three-quarters full with ice.

2 Add the tequila, cilantro leaves, triple sec, simple syrup, and pineapple juice. Shake *vigorously* to chill.

3 Strain the mixture into a tall glass filled with ice.

4 Top with soda water and stir to blend. Garnish.

CAIPIRINHA
MAKES 1

GLASS: Chilled old-fashioned or bistro
GARNISH: Mint sprig

While it hasn't yet achieved the superstardom of the Mojito, this Brazilian standard is making waves in trendy bars everywhere. Visit a Brazilian restaurant anywhere in the world and you'll find Caipirinhas being quaffed by expatriate Cariocas looking for the taste of home and anyone who likes a drink that packs a smooth punch.

Cachaça, like most other rums, is derived from the sugarcane plant. The major difference is that rum is made from molasses (a by-product of sugar refining) and Cachaça is made from fresh sugarcane juice (like Agricole rum) that's been fermented and distilled. It is produced almost exclusively in Brazil and imported, but is widely available now at most liquor stores.

½ lime, cut into thin wedges
1 tablespoon light brown sugar
½ ounce simple syrup (see page 14)
3 ounces Cachaça

1 **Put the lime pieces, sugar, and simple syrup in the bottom of a cocktail shaker. Use a muddler or the back of a spoon to grind the sugars and lime together until the lime juice has melted the brown sugar.**

2 **Top with a scoop of ice and the Cachaça. Shake *vigorously* and strain the drink into the chilled glass.**

3 **Add a couple of the ice cubes from the shaker to the glass and garnish.**

Lavender Lush, page 60

Orange Basil Mojito,
page 61

Deep summer is when laziness finds respectability. —SAM KEEN

LAVENDER LUSH
MAKES 1 • *Photograph on page 58*

GLASS: Tall
GARNISH: Lime wedge and lavender or mint sprig

The sexy, lavender hue of this drink gives you a hint of the delicate lavender flavor in the glass. The gin can be replaced with vodka. Without the alcohol, this is a great beverage for a baby shower or any time you want to serve an elegant, nonalcoholic refresher.

2 ounces delicate gin (like Hendrick's or Wet)

1 ounce blueberry juice

½ ounce lavender simple syrup (see page 14)

2 tablespoons frozen lemonade or limeade concentrate

Up to ¼ cup soda water

1 **In a tall glass, mix the gin, blueberry juice, lavender simple syrup, and frozen lemonade concentrate to blend.**

2 **Fill the glass to the top with ice. Add soda water and stir to blend. Garnish.**

ORANGE BASIL MOJITO

MAKES 1 • *Photograph on page 59*

GLASS: Tall
GARNISH: Orange peel twist

It's my good fortune that my close friend Susan Kaufman owns one of Seattle's best restaurants—Serafina. Their Orange Basil Mojito is the most popular drink at the bar during the summer. This is made at Serafina with orange-infused rum, which adds an astonishing bright citrus note (see "Infusing Spirits," page 102). However, it is delightful with standard light rum as well.

6 basil leaves, sliced

½ ounce simple syrup (see page 14)

1 ounce fresh lime juice

1½ ounces light Bacardi rum

Juice of ½ orange

Soda water

1 **In a pint shaker glass, muddle the basil leaves, syrup, and lime juice. Add the rum and orange juice and stir to blend.**

2 **Pour into a glass filled with ice and stir.**

3 **Top off with soda water. Garnish.**

ROSEMARY'S BABY
MAKES 1

GLASS: Tall
GARNISH: Rosemary sprig and lime wedge

Delicate pink as a newborn baby's bottom with the exotic hint of rosemary, this is one complex yet refreshing summer quaff.

1½ ounces Bombay Sapphire gin
½ ounce Cointreau
1 ounce cranberry juice
½ ounce fresh lime juice
½ ounce rosemary simple syrup (see page 14)
Soda water

1 Fill a cocktail shaker three-quarters full with ice.

2 Add the gin, Cointreau, cranberry juice, lime juice, and rosemary simple syrup. Shake to chill. Strain the drink into a tall glass filled with ice.

3 Top off with soda water. Garnish.

Some men are like glasses—to produce their finest tones you must keep them wet.
—SAMUEL TAYLOR COLERIDGE

ACAPULCO CLIFF HANGER
MAKES 1

GLASS: Tall
RIM: Spiced salt (1 teaspoon kosher salt, a generous pinch of ground cayenne pepper, and a small pinch of dried ground ginger mixed together)
GARNISH: Watermelon wedge

This is one of the great ways to include summer's quintessential fruit in a cocktail. It's also a tart, unusual way to enjoy tequila. The Acapulco is basically a watermelon margarita with a hint of chile heat.

1 cup seedless watermelon chunks

2 ounces tequila

1 ounce lemon simple syrup (see page 14)

1 ounce fresh lime juice

1 ounce Cointreau

Lime wedge

Soda water or ginger ale to top, optional

1 Puree the watermelon chunks in the blender and strain, for about ⅓ cup of puree.

2 In a tall glass, combine the watermelon puree, tequila, lemon simple syrup, lime juice, and Cointreau. Stir to mix.

3 Moisten the rim of the serving glass with a lime wedge and press the rim into the spiced salt. Fill with ice. (Reserve the lime wedge.)

4 Strain the puree mixture into the cocktail glass. Top with a splash of soda water or ginger ale if you like.

5 Squeeze the lime wedge on top. Garnish.

LEMON BREEZE
MAKES 1

Limoncello is certainly Italy's gift to the lemon-loving mixologist. I enjoy the flavor best if it's extremely cold, so I recommend keeping Limoncello in the freezer. A beautiful rosy hue and tart, quenching flavors make this a great beachside drink.

I have definitely enjoyed this with the optional Champagne when there was some on hand. Or make these drinks for a crowd and open a bottle just for the occasion.

1 ounce Limoncello liqueur (from the freezer)

1 ounce Grey Goose Le Citron vodka

2 ounces cranberry juice

1 ounce ruby red grapefruit juice

Splash of soda water or brut Champagne or Prosecco, optional

1 **Pour the Limoncello, vodka, cranberry juice, and grapefruit juice into an ice-filled glass.**

2 **Stir to mix and chill. Add soda or Champagne to taste. Garnish.**

 The Backyard Bartender

NEGRONI
MAKES 1

Named for an Italian count, this classic aperitif was created in Florence in the early 1900s. When I serve this at sunset, I can almost feel the count standing beside me admiring the view—and the cocktail.

1 ounce Campari

1 ounce gin

1 ounce sweet red vermouth

About 2 ounces soda water to top, optional

1 Pour the Campari, gin, and vermouth into a glass filled with ice. Toss in the orange peel and stir to mix.

2 Add soda water to top if you like.

Fuzzy Italian

The Backyard Bartender

BAREFOOT
MAKES 1

GLASS: Chilled goblet or tall
GARNISH: Fresh strawberry

Coconut, banana, and rum are classic partners. This reminds me of a tropical drink I might have had at an island bar anywhere in the world from Hawaii to Barbados—or Bali. Multiply this recipe to make a big batch for your next cookout.

2 tablespoons mashed bananas

½ ounce Kahlúa

1 ounce cream of coconut (like Coco Lopez)

1 ounce light rum

¼ cup diced papaya or strawberries

½ ounce crème de banane

½ cup ice

1 **Mix the mashed banana, Kahlúa, coconut cream, rum, papaya, crème de banane, and ice in a blender until smooth.**

2 **Pour into the chilled glass. Garnish.**

FUZZY
MAKES 1

GLASS: Chilled old-fashioned (or short tumbler)
GARNISH: Peach slice and a sprig of mint

The delicate pomegranate note of the trendy new Pama liqueur is perfectly balanced with a nip of bitterness from the Campari to make the Fuzzy a real thirst quencher.

1½ ounces Pama liqueur

1½ ounces vodka

½ ounce (1 tablespoon) Campari

Soda water

Lime wedge

1 **Fill the chilled glass with ice. Pour the Pama, vodka, and Campari into the glass and stir.**

2 **Add soda and stir again.**

3 **Squeeze the lime on top and drop into the glass. Garnish.**

CANTON GINGER ALE
MAKES 2

GLASS: Tall
GARNISH: Skewer of candied ginger and lime wheel

With only the Cointreau, this is a very refreshing, slightly spicy beverage that most people can gulp with no ill effects throughout a long picnic afternoon. Add the vodka to transform this into a full-fledged cocktail.

You will need cheesecloth to prepare the ginger-infused syrup that creates this drink's distinctive flavor. But this unusual cocktail is definitely worth the extra effort to make the ginger syrup and is well suited to being made in large batches for parties.

For the ginger syrup

½ cup peeled and minced fresh gingerroot

3 to 4 tablespoons brown sugar

½ cup boiling water

1 ounce fresh lime juice

1 ounce Cointreau

2 ounces Absolut Citron vodka or Grey Goose L'Orange, optional

1 cup soda water

1 **To make the ginger syrup: Puree the fresh ginger in a food processor or mortar and pestle. Put the pureed ginger and the sugar in a small bowl and cover with the boiling water. Stir to blend and melt; let steep for about 30 minutes, until cool (longer to intensify the flavor). Strain through cheesecloth; squeeze the mixture and twist the cloth to get all of the liquid into the bowl. This can be done up to 24 hours ahead and refrigerated in a sealed container.**

2 **Mix the ginger syrup, lime juice, and Cointreau (and vodka, if using).**

3 **Pour into tall glasses filled with ice. Add the soda and stir. Garnish.**

Omit the Cointreau and vodka for a refreshing and sophisticated nonalcoholic cooler.

PEACH TOUCAN
MAKES 4 TO 5

GLASS: Chilled goblet or hurricane
GARNISH: Fresh mint and peach wedge

There's something so summertime, campout appealing about a cocktail that uses a "can" as a measuring tool. Dump the frozen lemonade into the blender. Fill the same can with vodka, toss in two unpeeled peaches and voilà—peachy fun! And, with such a modest amount of alcohol per cocktail, this can be the perfect sipping beverage for a brunch or ladies' lunch. The vodka can be doubled for a more potent potable and the flavor will still remain lush.

1 6-ounce can of frozen lemonade concentrate

6 ounces vodka (measured in lemonade can)

2 whole, pitted peaches (or 1 cup diced mango or papaya)

4 or 5 fresh thyme leaves, optional

1 Fill the blender half full with ice and add the lemonade, vodka, and peaches. (Reserve 4 or 5 slices for garnish.)

2 Blend until smooth and frothy.

3 Pour into the chilled glasses. Garnish.

Aqua de Pepino (left) and
Aqua de Sandia

Alcohol Never
Came into It

These refreshing options are delicious any time alcohol would be unwanted, such as when serving pregnant moms, folks who don't drink and/or are on special diets, and, of course, kids. It's my feeling that these offerings should have just as much pizzazz as the recipes with alcohol.

(A number of the cocktail recipes found elsewhere in the book are delicious without the liquor called for in the ingredients list. These are indicated with a ⛱.)

It is an odd but universally held opinion that anyone who doesn't drink must be an alcoholic. —P.J. O'ROURKE

In Mexico, every street corner seems to host a vendor selling one of these simple, remarkably refreshing coolers. Likely due to Mexico's astounding array of lush and luscious fruits, most locals would still rather quench their thirst with one of these fresh concoctions than a soda. I think you'll feel the same. The bright flavor relies on perfectly ripe ingredients and good water. And what a great way to use up any *overbearing* cucumber vines.

The Basic Methodology:

Puree fruit and water. Strain. Add more water and a little sweetener. Chill in the refrigerator for 2 to 24 hours.

Agua de Sandia (Watermelon)

1 In a blender, puree 4 cups diced melon and 2 cups cold water.

2 Strain through a sieve into a large pitcher.

3 Add 3 more cups cold water, ¼ cup (or up to ¾ cup) simple syrup (see page 14), 2 to 3 tablespoons fresh lime juice, and a pinch of salt. Stir to blend. Add more simple syrup or water as needed for the fruit.

4 Serve well chilled with a wedge of lime or melon.

Agua de Pepino (Cucumber)

1 In a blender, puree 3 large peeled and chopped cucumbers with 1½ cups cold water.

2 Strain through a sieve into a large pitcher.

3 Add 3 to 4 more cups cold still or sparkling water, 3 to 4 tablespoons fresh lime juice, and about ¼ cup (or up to ¾ cup) simple syrup (see page 14). (A pinch of chili pepper or salt is also good in this.)

4 Serve well chilled with a slice of cucumber dusted with chili pepper.

Alcohol Never Came into It **71**

Agua de Tamarindo (Tamarind)

1 In a large pitcher, whisk together ⅓ cup tamarind pulp or paste, 6 cups cold water, and ⅔ cup simple syrup (see page 14).

2 Serve well chilled. Garnish with a strawberry, pineapple wedge, or mango slice.

Agua de Piña (Pineapple)

1 In a blender, puree 3 cups peeled and chopped pineapple, 2 cups cold water, and 5 to 8 basil leaves.

2 Strain into a large pitcher.

3 Stir in ¼ cup simple syrup (see page 14), 3 more cups cold water, and 1 to 2 tablespoons fresh lime juice. Add more simple syrup (up to ½ cup) as needed.

4 Serve well chilled. Garnish with a pineapple wedge and a sprig of basil or mint.

STRAWBERRY SHIRLEY

MAKES 1

A fresh update on every little girl's favorite. With a bright strawberry flavor, this is sophisticated enough for anyone looking for a cool summer drink.

Juice of 1 lemon
1 tablespoon sugar
2 teaspoons grenadine
8 to 10 ripe strawberries
⅔ cup 7-Up

1 In a blender, mix the lemon, sugar, grenadine, and strawberries until fairly smooth.

2 Pour into a glass with ice. Top with 7-Up and stir. Garnish.

SALTY PUPPY
MAKES 1

GLASS: Old-fashioned
RIM: Lemon or lime wedge and kosher salt/sugar (1 teaspoon kosher salt mixed with 1 teaspoon sugar)
GARNISH: Fresh mint

The sugar/salt rim on the Salty Puppy gives it a touch of complexity. As the name indicates, this is an alcohol-free interpretation of the popular Salty Dog.

3 ounces pink grapefruit juice

2 ounces blood orange (or passion fruit) juice

½ ounce simple syrup (see page 14)

Ginger ale or soda water

1 Rim the glass by wiping it with the wedge of lemon or lime. Then press the glass into a saucer of the salt/sugar mixture.

2 Fill the glass with ice. Add the grapefruit and blood orange juice along with the simple syrup. Stir.

3 Top with a splash of ginger ale or soda water. Garnish.

PLAYFUL PIÑA
MAKES 1

GLASS: Margarita or wine
GARNISH: Pineapple wedge and a baby orchid

I love to serve this drink for brunch. It's elegant and with all this fruity flavor, no one misses the booze.

3 ounces pineapple juice

1 ounce cream of coconut (like Coco Lopez)

⅓ cup fresh berries or diced mango

1 cup crushed ice

1 Blend the pineapple juice, cream of coconut, fresh berries, and ice in a blender until smooth. Pour into the glass, garnish, and serve immediately.

Bloody Mary,
page 80

7 COCKTAILS
FOR A CROWD

You will definitely want to serve one of these recipes when you're having a crowd for cocktails. Instead of frantically shaking or stirring to order, coolly pour guests something lovely from a pitcher. These recipes were selected both because of their universal popularity (necessary when you're serving one flavor to everyone) and because of the beautiful presentation they make. BTW, always have mineral water and some wine on hand, as well.

Set up the pitcher (or punch bowl) on a table surrounded by glasses already dressed with the appropriate garnish and you've not only solved the cocktail crunch but also created a handsome centerpiece. The one challenge is keeping things icy cold—this is critical. Start with all ingredients well chilled (especially the alcohol). Consider preparing some creatively flavored ice (see page 44) and/or resting the pitcher in a larger bowl of ice. Plain ice cubes in the pitcher should be the chilling method of last resort.

BLOODY MARY
MAKES 8 (ABOUT 7 CUPS)
Photograph on page 78

GLASS: Goblet or tall
RIM: Lime wedge and 1 teaspoon celery salt mixed with 1 teaspoon kosher salt
GARNISH: Celery, green onion, pickled green beans, and cilantro

Serve this for brunch, breakfast, the morning after, or to cool off around the pool—this spicy drink is always welcome. The vegetable "salad" that garnishes it is fun and may provide a little necessary nourishment for a recovering reveler, too. Be sure to start the preparations for this well ahead of time to allow for refrigeration.

1 can (46 ounces) V-8 vegetable juice

3 tablespoons grated fresh horseradish (or ¼ cup prepared, drained)

1 teaspoon celery salt

2 tablespoons Worcestershire sauce

1 teaspoon Tabasco sauce, or to taste

3 tablespoons fresh orange juice

Juice of 2 limes

12 twists from a pepper mill of black pepper

1½ to 2½ cups vodka

Chipped ice, for serving

Lime wedges, for serving

1 In a blender, combine the vegetable juice, horseradish, celery salt, Worcestershire sauce, Tabasco sauce, orange juice, lime juice, and pepper. Mix well.

2 Cover and refrigerate for at least 6 hours (or up to 2 days) before serving.

3 Moisten the glass rims with lime juice and press into a saucer of the celery salt mixture to coat.

4 To serve, put the pitcher on the buffet surrounded by the already-rimmed glasses. Place a bucket of chipped ice, a bowl of lime wedges, the garnishes, a bottle of vodka, and a jigger nearby with the following printed directions:

"Fill glass with ice, add 1 to 2 jiggers of vodka and top with juice mix. Stir to blend and add one or all of the garnishes."

The Backyard Bartender

PIMM'S CUP
MAKES 10

GLASS: Rocks, tall, or goblet
GARNISH: Finely sliced orange, lemon, cucumber, and apple (2 of each), plus lots of fresh mint

Pimm's No. 1 is a low-octane (50-proof) fragrant liquor made with gin that has been infused with fruits, spices, and herbs. Because of its relatively low alcohol content, and the veritable fruit salad that typically accompanies it, this is a drink that is well suited to long, hot afternoons of sipping without getting sloshed. Several glasses of properly mixed Pimm's will leave you refreshed yet still ambulatory even if consumed under the midday sun that Englishmen were said to crave.

3 cups Pimm's No. 1, well chilled

3 cups lemonade (preferably homemade), well chilled

3 cups 7-Up or ginger ale, well chilled (or replace the 7-Up with champagne for a snazzy, tasty twist)

1 Combine the **Pimm's No. 1**, lemonade, and 7-Up or ginger ale in a large pitcher.

2 Add about half of the garnish elements to the pitcher and put the rest in a chilled bowl on the side for guests to add to their individual ice-filled glasses.

GINGER BLUSH MARTINI
MAKES 8

GLASS: Chilled martini
RIM: Ginger sugar (3 tablespoons sugar and ¾ teaspoon ground ginger)
GARNISH: Lime wedges

The fresh ginger flavor of this martini is a subtle surprise that blends the lime and vodka together seamlessly. This cocktail really elicits a *wow* from guests. And, as a friend of mine suggested, all of that ginger would probably settle an upset stomach, too. Serve this before a meal of Asian flavors. For another great pitcher drink, try this recipe with fine tequila in place of the vodka.

8 ounces (1 cup) fresh lime juice

4 ounces (½ cup) triple sec

2 ounces ginger syrup (see page 14)

16 ounces (2 cups) premium vodka (like Grey Goose or Ketel One)

1 In a large pitcher, combine the lime juice, triple sec, ginger syrup, and vodka. Cover and chill for 1 to 2 hours.

2 On a flat saucer, combine the sugar and ginger. Rub a lime wedge around the rims of the glasses to moisten. Press the rims into the saucer of ginger sugar.

3 To serve, add lots of ice to the pitcher and stir for 30 to 40 seconds to chill thoroughly. Immediately strain the very cold liquid into the glasses. Garnish.

MANGO-LIME SANGRIA

MAKES 8

GLASS: Goblet or wine
GARNISH: Fresh lavender or mint

Mangos are definitely a favorite fruit for many of us. Using mangos here with dry rosé, instead of the more classic red wine, makes this a lighter, more refreshing sangria that is perfect for summer's heat.

- 1 cup peeled, chopped mango (or apricot)
- ⅓ cup superfine sugar (which may be purchased or made by grinding regular sugar in a spice grinder)
- 10 ounces fresh orange juice
- 10 ounces fresh lime juice
- 1 ounce triple sec
- 3 limes, thinly sliced
- ⅓ cup peach brandy or peach schnapps
- 1 to 2 bottles dry rosé (like Angoves Nine Vine or Barnard Griffin Sangiovese Rosé)
- 2 trays of ice cubes with a raspberry or rose petal in each (see page 44 for more ice art ideas), optional
- 1 to 2 cups soda water

1 Combine the chopped mango and sugar and let sit for 1 hour at room temperature.

2 Combine the macerated mango, orange juice, lime juice, triple sec, sliced limes, peach brandy, and rosé in a large (preferably clear) pitcher. Stir to blend. Cover and refrigerate for 30 to 60 minutes (or up to 8 hours).

3 To serve, stir to mix. Fill glasses one-half full of ice cubes; add the juice mixture and soda water to taste. Stir. Garnish.

IPANEMA PUNCH

MAKES 12

GLASS: Tall or punch cup
GARNISH: Mint leaves and 12 pineapple
wedges

All of the flavors of the tropics make an
appearance in this sensational, lemon-hued
punch—banana, rum, pineapple, and
orange. Serve this at a BBQ featuring great
pork ribs.

½ cup Cointreau

2 cups light rum

3 ounces crème de banane

1 cup pink grapefruit juice

2 cups fresh orange juice

½ cup fresh lime juice

1 cup pineapple juice

36 frozen whole strawberries or raspberries

3 to 4 cups ginger ale

1 In a large bowl, combine the Cointreau, rum,
crème de banane, grapefruit juice, orange juice,
lime juice, and pineapple juice. Cover and chill
for at least 1 hour or overnight.

2 Pour the mixture into a punch bowl or large
pitcher. Add the frozen berries (as "ice cubes").

3 Top with ginger ale and stir gently to blend.
Garnish each glass.

Man, being reasonable, must get drunk. The best of life is but intoxication. —LORD BYRON

COSMOPOLITAN SUNSET
MAKES 6

GLASS: Chilled martini
GARNISH: Lime wheels

Freezing the rosy cranberry juice into cubes keeps this cocktail cool on the buffet without diluting its potency with plain ice cubes. The cranberry ice cubes also create a pretty "sunset" pattern as they melt. I'm a huge fan of pomegranate juice in cooking. If you can find it, I think it's a sophisticated alternative to the cranberry juice.

9 ounces cranberry or pomegranate juice

12 ounces premium vodka (like Absolut Citron or Grey Goose Le Citron)

4 ounces fresh lime juice

4 ounces Cointreau

1 **Pour half of the cranberry juice into an ice cube tray and freeze.**

2 **In a large, clear pitcher, combine the remaining cranberry juice, vodka, lime juice, and Cointreau. Cover and chill for at least 1 hour.**

3 **To serve immediately, put 1 cranberry ice cube in each glass. Add a lime wheel to each. Pour the vodka blend into the glasses and stir. Or to serve on the buffet for a few minutes, add the cranberry ice cubes to the pitcher. Set out a bowl of lime wheels and allow guests to serve themselves.**

 The Backyard Bartender

MOJITOS FOR A CROWD
MAKES 8

GLASS: Old-fashioned or tall
GARNISH: Lime/mint ice cubes, lime wedges, and reserved mint sprigs

This cocktail has been the national drink of Cuba for more than one hundred years. As of late, it seems to have enrolled most of the United States, too. Its sprightly combination of tons of fresh mint and lime makes it a sensation any time the weather is hot. There are lots of delicious variations out there now (see our Orange Basil Mojito on page 61), but this recipe is the classic—the inspiration for all of the others.

To make this practical to serve to a crowd, the basic mixture can be prepared several hours before the party and held in the refrigerator.

¾ cup fresh lime juice

1 bunch (about 50 leaves) mint, washed and dried plus 8 pretty sprigs for garnish

½ cup sugar

1½ to 2 cups light rum (like Bacardi)

Cracked ice

1½ cups soda water

1 Pour ¼ cup of lime juice into an ice cube tray. Add a perfect little mint leaf to each slot and freeze. Chill a pretty, clear pitcher for at least half an hour.

2 Combine most of the rest of the mint (reserving a handful) and the sugar in a heavy 4-cup bowl. Use a wooden spoon or muddler to "muddle" them together (e.g., crush the mint and the sugar together into a paste until the mint is aromatic).

3 Stir in the remaining lime juice and rum. Mix until the sugar is completely dissolved. Let rest for at least 10 minutes in the refrigerator. (The drink can be prepared up to this step several hours ahead, covered, and kept in the refrigerator.)

4 Strain the mixture into the chilled pitcher. Add the mint-decorated ice cubes and an extra "handful" of mint. Stir to mix. This can sit out for up to 20 minutes.

5 To serve, pour about ⅓ cup of the Mojito mixture into a glass filled with crushed ice, top with soda water, and stir. Garnish with a mint sprig and a lime wedge.

Bellinitini, page 88

8 | SPARKLERS

Champagne and other sparkling wines, like Prosecco and Cava, are wonderful at any time of year. For heaven's sake, you practically couldn't hold New Year's Eve without one. However, the crisp, effervescent character of sparkling wine really seems to hit the spot on hot summer days. Champagne is soothing on its own, served crispy cold in a graceful flute, and even more special used in one of the following fizzy cocktails.

With the rush of summer weddings, this chapter offers just the thing when you're looking for that special cocktail that will make your reception or engagement party feel unique.

Fighting is like Champagne. It goes to the heads of cowards as quickly as of heroes. —MARGARET MITCHELL

BELLINITINI

MAKES 1 ● *Photograph on page 86*

GLASS: Chilled flute or martini
GARNISH: Fresh raspberry or peach slice

The classic flavors of the Bellini get a little beefing up from orange-flavored vodka. This is an intriguing, fizzy martini.

1 ounce orange-flavored vodka
(like Grey Goose L'Orange)

1 ounce peach or apricot nectar
(like Looza)

3 ounces cold brut Champagne
or dry sparkling wine

1 **Mix the vodka and peach nectar in a shaker with lots of ice.**

2 **Strain the mixture into the chilled glass and top with the cold Champagne.**

3 **Stir once. Garnish.**

FRENCH MINT
MAKES 1

Brandy and Champagne are a classic pairing. Here refreshing mint syrup is added to create a bubbly take on the summer flavors of a mint julep.

1 ounce brandy

2 teaspoons mint simple syrup (see page 14)

½ cup cold brut Champagne or dry sparkling wine

1 Place the brandy and mint simple syrup in a shaker with ice.

2 Shake to chill. Strain the mixture into a glass.

3 Top with Champagne and stir once. Garnish.

Mediterraneano,
page 92

A perfect summer day is when the sun is shining, the breeze is blowing, the birds are singing and the lawn mower is broken. —JAMES DENT

THE LAWN MOWER

MAKES 2

GLASS: Chilled martini or flute
GARNISH: Melon balls and mint leaves on a skewer

Delicate melon, mint, and a hint of vanilla make this into a silky textured refresher. The Lawn Mower would be perfect at an engagement party or as a signature drink at a summer wedding.

1 cup diced, ripe honeydew, cantaloupe, or seedless watermelon

1 ounce premium vanilla vodka (like Stoli Vanil)

½ ounce Cointreau

¾ ounce fresh lime juice

1 tablespoon roughly chopped fresh mint

About ½ cup cold brut Champagne or dry sparkling wine

1 **Puree the melon in a blender (add 1 or 2 tablespoons of water if necessary).**

2 **Press the melon mixture through a strainer into a cocktail shaker filled with ice.**

3 **Add the vodka, Cointreau, lime juice, and mint. Shake *vigorously* to infuse.**

4 **Strain the mixture into the chilled glasses and top with Champagne float.**

5 **Stir once. Garnish.**

MEDITERRANEANO
MAKES 1 • *Photograph on page 90*

GLASS: Flute
GARNISH: Orange peel twist

All of the sunny flavors of the Mediterranean, along with the bite of Campari, turn this Champagne cocktail into a complex and refreshing treat. This is definitely an adult beverage suitable to serve in place of a martini or a Manhattan.

Sugar cube
1 to 2 dashes Angostura bitters
2 teaspoons ruby red grapefruit juice
2 teaspoons Campari
2 tablespoons Pama liqueur
½ cup cold brut Champagne (or sparkling wine or sparkling water)

1 Moisten the sugar cube with a dash or two of bitters and drop the cube into the bottom of the glass.

2 Add the grapefruit juice, Campari, and Pama and stir to mix.

3 Gently pour in the Champagne and stir once. Garnish with the orange peel twist and perhaps a pink elephant.

LA VIE EN ROSE
CHAMPAGNE COCKTAIL
MAKES 2

GLASS: Flute
RIM: 2 tablespoons superfine sugar (which may be purchased or made by grinding regular sugar in a spice grinder)
GARNISH: Orange wheel or a fresh cherry

Make any party sparkle with this romantic, rose-tinted cocktail. Prepare the juice component ahead, then just add the Champagne at party time. This would be perfect to offer guests as they arrive at a wedding reception.

¾ ounce fresh lime juice

1½ ounces Cointreau

1½ ounces cranberry juice

1 cup chilled brut Champagne or dry sparkling wine

1 Mix the lime juice, **Cointreau**, and cranberry juice in a pitcher. Chill, covered, for at least 2 hours or overnight.

2 Moisten the rim of a glass with water and dip it into a saucer of sugar to coat.

3 Pour the juice mixture into the glasses and add ½ cup **Champagne** to each. Stir once gently. Garnish.

Chocolate-Dipped
Banana, page 96

9 | **DESSERT** IN A GLASS

In the course of developing all of these enticing cocktails, some recipes emerged that were too wonderful to leave out but that seemed to cross over the line between a cocktail-hour beverage and a postdinner indulgence. A chapter on desserts in a glass was my solution for keeping these delicious drinks in the book and letting you know where they fit on your menu.

Mocha Frappé, page 101

CHOCOLATE-DIPPED
BANANA
MAKES 2 • *Photograph on page 94*

GLASS: Soda or milkshake
RIM: Orange wedge and Nesquik or dark brown sugar
GARNISH: Fresh or maraschino cherry

Remember the incredible indulgence of walking along the boardwalk or shore with a frozen banana on a stick that had been dipped in chocolate just for you? Well, this frothy concoction comes pretty close to replicating that quintessential summer experience. Dive in.

1½ ounces crème de cacao or Godiva liqueur (dark)

1 ounce dark rum, like Myers's

1½ ounces Stoli Vanil vodka (or homemade, see page 102)

1 cup softened French vanilla ice cream

½ cup chopped, ripe banana

1 cup cracked ice

¾ cup chilled cream soda

1 **Moisten the rim of the glass with the orange wedge and press the rim into a saucer of Nestlé Quik to coat.**

2 **In a blender, puree all the ingredients except the cream soda. Then stir in the soda.**

3 **Pour into the glasses. Garnish. Serve with giant straws.**

The Backyard Bartender

NECTARINES 'N' CREAM
MAKES 2

GLASS: Chilled brandy snifter or margarita
GARNISH: Nutmeg and nectarine slice

Amaretto (that luscious almond liqueur from Italy) and nectarines are absolutely elegant together. Serve amaretti or biscotti alongside for a special summer ice-cream dessert.

¼ cup Amaretto

1 ripe nectarine or peach, pitted

2 scoops premium vanilla or peach ice cream

1 **Blend the Amaretto, nectarine, and ice cream until creamy and smooth.**

2 **Pour the mixture into the glasses.**

3 **Sprinkle with nutmeg and garnish.**

THE BLEND TREND

Frozen or blended drinks became trendy in the 1950s with the introduction of a blender to nearly every suburban kitchen. People were endlessly fascinated by the possibilities for creating frothy, cool, ice-cream-*floaty* kinds of drinks.

Blended drinks typically appeal to those who are looking for something light, perhaps sweet, and not too heavy on the alcohol. Nearly any ripe summer fruit can be whipped up with some liquor and ice to create a warm-weather treat—the epitome of summer in a glass. If you have lots of strawberries or melon on hand, use the recipes in this chapter to create your own house specialty.

If you plan to make a party-sized batch of a blended drink, put the alcohol in the freezer ahead of time to help things stay extra cold. Adding more ice to the blender will create a more solid, less slushy texture.

Pomegranate Freeze, page 100

Ginger Snow Martini,
page 101

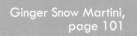

POMEGRANATE FREEZE
MAKES 6 TO 8 • *Photograph on page 98*

GLASS: Chilled martini or dessert
GARNISH: Fresh strawberry or lemon zest
(or pomegranate seeds in season)

Granita, a traditional summer treat in Italy and France, is a mixture of sugar, liquid (like fruit juice, coffee, or wine), and water that is stirred while freezing; this creates the fine, granular quality of the finished ice. In this recipe, the combination of Pama pomegranate liqueur and Champagne becomes the ultimate granita cocktail. Granita can be prepared up to two days ahead and stored, covered, in the freezer. "Rake" it briefly to loosen before serving.

1 cup (6 ounces) small strawberries, washed and hulled

1 cup and 1 tablespoon simple syrup (see page 14)

¾ cup Pama liqueur, plus more for drizzling

1½ cups chilled brut Champagne

1 **Puree the strawberries in a blender or food processor.**

2 **In a large bowl, whisk ¾ cup of the puree and the simple syrup. Mix in the Pama, then the Champagne.**

3 **Pour the mixture into an 8-inch-square metal baking pan.**

4 **Freeze the mixture until it is icy around the edges, about 45 minutes. Use a fork to rake the frozen edges toward the center. Repeat the raking into the center every 30 minutes, until frozen through, about 5 hours total.**

5 **Cover and keep frozen.**

6 **To serve, use a large spoon or small ice-cream scoop to mold and serve in the frosty martini glasses. Garnish with the fruit and drizzle with chilled Pama.**

 The Backyard Bartender

GINGER SNOW MARTINI

MAKES 8 • *Photograph on page 99*

GLASS: Chilled martini, margarita, or dessert coupe
GARNISH: Fresh mint sprigs and fresh berries

This is one of the most stunning cocktails I've ever served, not to mention a sensational summer dessert. The gingery bite of the granita marries superbly with the floral citrus notes of the Hendrick's. Unexpected and exceptional!

If you don't want to prepare eight cocktails at once, the granita will last in your freezer (well wrapped) for at least ten days—use it at will.

1 bottle brut Champagne or sparkling wine

2 to 3 teaspoons peeled and grated fresh gingerroot

6 tablespoons sugar

2 tablespoons lemon zest

8 ounces Hendrick's (or other premium) gin

1. **To make the ginger-granita "snow" (this recipe makes 4 cups of it), put the Champagne, ginger, sugar, and lemon zest into a heavy saucepan and bring just to a boil over medium heat, stirring constantly. Remove from heat and cool to room temperature.**

2. **Pour the mixture into an 8-inch-square metal baking pan.**

3. **Freeze the mixture until it is icy around the edges, about 45 minutes. Use a fork to rake the frozen edges toward the center. Repeat the raking into the center every 30 minutes, until frozen through, about 5 hours total.**

4. **Cover and keep frozen.**

5. **To serve, use a large spoon or small ice-cream scoop to mold the "snow" in the chilled glasses. Top each glass with 1 ounce of chilled gin. Garnish.**

MOCHA FRAPPÉ

MAKES 2 • *Photograph on page 95*

GLASS: Coffee mug or pilsner
GARNISH: Nutmeg, cinnamon, or chocolate shavings

Designed for diehard coffee-heads, this duplicates your favorite coffee-bar treat—with a kick. Make pitchers of these for your next Sunday brunch.

½ cup chilled double-strength coffee or espresso

2 small scoops vanilla ice cream

2 ounces Stoli Vanil vodka (or homemade, see page 102)

1 ounce Kahlúa

½ ounce dark chocolate liqueur (like Godiva)

1. **Put the coffee, ice cream, vodka, Kahlúa, and dark chocolate liqueur into a blender and process until frothy.**

2. **Pour the mixture into the glasses, garnish, and serve with a big straw.**

INFUSING SPIRITS

Infusing spirits with custom flavors is a concept that has become all the rage on the bar scene. The recent enthusiasm for cocktails (really not seen since Prohibition and then the '50s) has brought chefs and others with cooking sensibilities into the cocktail design arena. Looking for more ways in which to "infuse" ever-fresher and more-complex flavor notes into their cocktails, they began to experiment with creating their own special spirits. Steeping fresh ingredients in white liquor allows just that—often with delicious, seductive, and very personal results.

Of course, major high-end manufacturers are doing this, too. Stoli, Absolut, Grey Goose, and Bacardi have a raft of excellent flavor profiles available in their spirit lines.

CREATE A SIGNATURE VODKA, RUM, OR GIN

Vodka is the liquor most often infused because of the clean palate it provides. However, light rum or noncomplex gins may be handled in a similar fashion. Following are some general guidelines and suggestions for infusing to get you started on the creation of your own unique flavored spirits. Experiment with one of these and then let your imagination take you from there.

INFUSING

Put the selected flavoring in a clean glass jar, top with the spirit, and seal. Let steep at room temperature for at least 2 days before tasting. Note: Soft-leaved herbs, like basil and mint, will need to be watched more closely as they may be ready after only 36 hours.

Shake or stir once a day. After the first 2 days, taste once a day to see how the flavors are developing. Sample the brew both "neat" (straight and unchilled) and "on the rocks." Continue to intensify the flavor by letting the mixture infuse for up to 2 weeks at room temperature.

When the desired flavor profile is reached, strain the spirit immediately and discard the infusion ingredients. Filter the spirit through a cheesecloth and store another 1 to 2 weeks at room temperature to allow flavors to meld. Then transfer to the refrigerator. Many of these recipes take on a lovely, appealing hue from their flavoring ingredients. Filter through cheesecloth as necessary to retain clarity.

The strained, infused spirit will keep for up to 6 months in the refrigerator in a well-sealed glass jar or bottle.

Wash and dry all infusion ingredients before using.

◆ 2 cups fresh fruit in large chunks (peaches, apricots, or pears) or berries

◆ 2 fresh vanilla beans, split lengthwise

◆ 1 cup peeled and chopped pineapple
   1 split vanilla bean
   1 tablespoon light honey

◆ 3 Meyer lemons, finely sliced
   1 tablespoon mild honey

◆ ⅓ cup whole coffee beans
   1 split vanilla bean

◆ ⅓ cup peeled and chopped fresh gingerroot
   1 finely sliced orange
   1 tablespoon mild honey

◆ ¼ cup slightly crushed basil or mint leaves
   (strain after 1½ to 2 days)

HOT PEPPER (OR CAJUN KICKER) INFUSION

The Cajun Kicker is a little different from the above infusions because the capsaicin in chiles is very volatile and can quickly overspice your spirit. (I recommend aging this in the refrigerator.)

This is a great way for those of you who enjoy the endorphin rush from chile peppers in your food to get some into your cocktails, too.

   2 to 3 fresh Thai peppers
   2 fresh jalapeño peppers
   ½ red bell pepper, sliced

1 Wear gloves while handling the chiles. Gently pierce the Thai and jalapeño peppers with a knife tip.

2 Add all of the peppers to your container of spirit (tequila can be good here), seal, and refrigerate to age. Taste after 3 days (don't even think about leaving the peppers in the spirit for more than a week!).

3 Strain and refrigerate as you would with the other infusions.

ORANGE-INFUSED RUM

These instructions come from Chris Bollenbacher, the "infusion master" at Serafina restaurant in Seattle. This is the rum he prepares and uses in his Orange Basil Mojito (see page 61).

   4 oranges
   1 750-milliliter bottle Bacardi light rum
   Honey to taste

1 Remove the zest from all 4 oranges and reserve.

2 Juice one of the oranges to yield about ¼ cup of juice.

3 Remove all skin and membranes from the flesh of the 3 remaining oranges.

4 Combine the orange zest, orange juice, orange segments, rum, and honey in a jar; close tightly. Store at room temperature for 1½ to 2 weeks (taste occasionally to test for desired flavor intensity).

5 Filter the rum through cheesecloth and store another 1 to 2 weeks at room temperature to allow flavors to meld. Again, taste occasionally to test for desired flavor intensity. Filter through cheesecloth as necessary to keep the clarity. This rum will keep for up to 6 months well sealed in the refrigerator.

GLOSSARY OF
COCKTAIL TALK

APERITIF An alcoholic drink (typically with low alcohol content) meant to be consumed before lunch or dinner to stimulate the appetite (and the conversation). Aperitifs are also often used as ingredients in mixed drinks. Popular aperitifs include Campari, Lillet, and Dubonnet.

BITTERS As their name suggests, bitters are a bitter additive made from dozens, if not hundreds, of herbs, spices, and plants. Bitters are often used to flavor cocktails (the Sazerac and Manhattan rely on bitters for their classic flavor profile). Use bitters in moderation, as too much can ruin the cocktail. Angostura is the most common type, but Peychaud, orange, and peach are flavorful variations to experiment with.

BRUISING This term is most often employed when talking about a shaken gin martini. *Bruising* describes the result of vigorously shaking the gin and ice together. After being strained into the martini glass, tiny shards of ice will float on the surface of the gin, creating a pattern. Some feel this releases the flavor of the gin. Those who dislike bruising prefer a *stirred* martini.

COCKTAIL An alcoholic drink, usually served chilled. A cocktail should contain no more than 2 to 3 ounces of alcohol and no more than five (maybe six) ingredients. The drink shouldn't have more than about 9 ounces of liquid altogether.

DIRTY A dirty martini has a little bit of olive brine added to it.

DRY In the cocktail realm, this term is typically employed in reference to a martini or a Manhattan. In both cases, this refers to the amount of vermouth in the recipe—a *dry* martini has only a small amount of vermouth. As more vermouth is added, the martini becomes *wetter*. A dry Manhattan has only dry (white) vermouth and no sweet (red) vermouth.

INFUSE Spirits may be flavored via infusing or steeping with an unlimited array of herbs, fruits, spices, or vegetables. Typically infusing is done with vodka or rum.

JIGGER A bar measure. A jigger or some measuring tool is essential to the creation of correct and, therefore, sublime cocktails (see "Tools of the Mixologist" on page 14).

LIQUEUR *Liqueur* is defined as a spirit that has been sweetened and flavored (often brandy or rum). Flavorings include herbs, fruits, nuts, spices, or a combination. Popular liqueurs include Grand Marnier, Amaretto, and Kahlúa. Liqueurs are also delicious drizzled over fresh fruit or ice cream for a super-easy dessert.

NEAT Alcohol that is served straight with no mixer and no ice. Usually in a shot glass.

ON THE ROCKS A drink served on a generous amount of ice (rocks).

Gin, as a category, is experiencing an explosion of creativity. In the past, its bone dry, perfumey profile has made it a love-it-or-hate-it spirit (with an awful lot of folks in the *hate-it* camp). However, starting about five years ago, new gins began to appear with less predictable and more roundly appealing flavor notes: Hendrick's, which lists rose petals among its botanicals; Tanqueray No. Ten, which uses whole fruits rather than citrus zest; Wet from Beefeater, which is flavored with pears. And there are many more varieties from artisanal makers, like Aviation, which have added delicate complexity to the essentially botanical and citrusy notes of gin. Most professional mixologists cite gin as their favorite spirit. Try it—you just might like one of these brands.

PART   A *part* refers to the relative amount of an ingredient. It is *not* a fixed amount. For example, if a recipe calls for 1 part A and 2 parts B, then the final drink should have twice as much B as it does A. In this way, drinks can be made as large as necessary. Many classic cocktail recipes are written in this fashion.

RIMMED GLASS   The lip or edge of the glass is moistened and pressed into a flavored coating, such as cinnamon sugar, to add another layer of flavor to the cocktail. (The exception to the wetting then dipping technique is when simply coating the rim with a liquid like melted chocolate—yum!)

RINSE   Many recipes call for a glass to be *rinsed* with a liquid (often vermouth) before the remaining ingredients are added. To rinse glasses, add the liquid to a glass that has been chilled first. Swirl to coat the inside and then pour the liquid into a second glass and so on. After all the glasses have been coated in this way, discard any remaining liquid and pour the chilled cocktail into them.

SHAKEN COCKTAIL All ingredients are placed in a cocktail shaker with lots of cubed ice. The goal here is to employ *vigorous* wrist action in the creation of the marvelous tinkly, sparkly sound of a handmade cocktail. You will also be mixing and cooling your ingredients before drizzling them into the lucky recipient's glass (see Techniques of the Mixologist on page 12).

SIMPLE SYRUP Sugar is dissolved in water over heat to create a sweetener that mixes easily with cold liquids (see page 14 for an array of flavored simple syrup recipes).

SPARKLING WINE Nothing can take its place for a celebratory toast or as a complement to a creamy dessert. True Champagne comes only from a particular region of France. But there are excellent sparkling wines from many other parts of the world: Prosecco from Italy, Cava from Spain, and fine examples from the United States, such as Domaine Chandon and Schramsberg. Don't chill sparkling wine until planning to serve it.

STIR For those who dislike shaking their martinis, add the ingredients to an ice-filled pitcher and stir. The goal here is to mix and chill the ingredients in a gentle, non-confrontational way. Those who fear *bruising* their gin prefer this method.

STRAIGHT UP A *straight-up* (or just *up*) drink has no ice. It's really the opposite of *on the rocks*. This would describe all martinis.

TWIST A twist is a garnish made from the rind of a lemon or lime (usually a lemon) using a channel knife. The longer it is (like Grandpa's impressive skein of apple peel), the more appealing (see Techniques and Tools of the Mixologist, page 12).

ACKNOWLEDGMENTS

I would like to begin by thanking my stalwart agent, Susan Ginsburg, for bringing this immensely enjoyable project to me. She continues to refashion an agent's role in a collaborative style all her own.

Thanks also to my assistant, Sue Zuehlsdorff, who bravely slogged alongside me through day after day of "imbibing-for-a-cause" while retaining her equilibrium and good sense. To my friend and talented food stylist Martha Gooding, who styled the cocktails while holding my hand throughout the shoot and the visualization leading up to it. To Patt Davis, pal and coincidentally a grand proofreader, who used her sharp pencil to help fine-tune the manuscript.

As this project evolved, many friends and colleagues jumped on board to offer their expertise and opinions about cocktails—and it turns out, nearly everyone has some. I'd like to thank Ryan Magarian, Lisa Dupar, Cynthia Nims, and Susan Kaufman (along with her great bar staff at Serafina). Also, Marta Magnoni, a wonderful client, mentor, and friend who provided editorial expertise and insight about just how this book should look. Gratitude also to Bob Paulinski, MW, my mentor in all things spirited.

Many thanks to Sur La Table, with whom I've had a longtime relationship of the very best kind, who stepped up for this project and provided a bounty of their beautiful glasses and bar equipment to grace these pages.

Aliza Fogelson, my editor at Clarkson Potter, was a pleasure to collaborate with. Loaded with creative ideas and an open mind, she helped shape *The Backyard Bartender* right from the start. And photographer Colleen Duffley, who brought her talented camera and knowledge of Florida locations to this project, creating some truly inviting visions of the cocktail.

Thanks to the owners of Lollygag House in Grayton Beach, Florida (www.emeraldcoasttours.com/186banfillstreet) for allowing us to stay in their gorgeous beachfront home during the shoot. We also used Lollygag as the setting for many of the pictures. Thanks also to the following Florida Gulf Coast shops who contributed unique props and glassware for the photos: Flavors of France, Gourd Garden Courtyard, Craft, and Pizitz Home and Cottage.

Finally, *muchas gracias* to the generous liquor distributors who provided us with their potent products: Ed Knutel of Bacardi USA, Ralph Kennedy of Moët Hennessy US, Mike Dieckhus of William Grant, and Mike Sporich of Heaven Hill Distilleries.

Salud!

INDEX

Mojitos for a Crowd, page 85

The Willamette, page 32